THINGS
I CAN'T
EXPLAIN

STEP INTO MY WORLD

ASIA CARRACTER

Things I Can't Explain

GROWING UP ON the west side of Jacksonville, Florida, I never imagined that one day I would write and publish a book. When I was a kid, I was shy. I wasn't outgoing and didn't like to talk much. I spent a lot of time alone, and like a lot of shy kids, my best friends were books. I loved to read, both fiction and nonfiction. Books let me have new experiences and adventures, and they also gave me an example of how to work through my own issues. I started getting to know myself better by writing down my thoughts and feelings, and I realized I had an opportunity to help others by writing a book, just like books had helped me.

My life looked perfect. I had everything a child could want, including my own room. Although we moved a few times when I was growing up, going between apartments, we always lived in safe neighborhoods, and my life was stable. But part of what I want you to understand is that even when life looks good from the outside, it can be more complicated than that. It's not your family's job to figure out your life—you have to do that for yourself. This book is about how I got involved in some major drama and how I pulled myself out of it to have a better future.

As I've said, my life was good. I had everything I wanted. But I was missing something I really needed: a genuinely present and caring father. Like most kids, I took my parents at face value until I was old enough to observe and understand things on my own. For me, my big awakening to reality happened when I was around fourteen and started noticing more about my dad. In some ways, he was strong and admirable. He took care of housing for me and my mom and sister, and he was always giving money to my mom.

He was a good provider, but the flip side of that is that he was a hustler. On top of that, he was ridiculously strict. There were clothes he wouldn't allow us to wear, hairstyles he wouldn't let us have, and he wouldn't even allow us to wear nail polish. He was overprotective in those ways, which I came to see as hypocritical, because when it came to women, he could be very abusive. He was in and out of jail, and I still don't really know why, although from rumors I heard and just what I observed of him, I'm pretty sure it was for rape and assault. Nobody came right out and told me, and some part of me didn't want to know, so I didn't ask.

I knew what I saw at home, though. He put my mother through hell, and I knew he was capable of beating on people. He never did it in front of me, but just knowing he had done it was enough to change how I felt about him. My feelings about my dad were complex and difficult. I was sad and angry. I wanted to rebel against his unnecessary rules, but at the same time, looking back, I wish I'd had a real relationship with him where he gave me actual guidance like a parent should, rather than arbitrary rules that didn't mean anything and just made me want to defy him.

My mother is the sweetest mama ever—anyone would love to have a mama like her. She would break her back for me and my sister, and I love her to death because no matter what we decided in life, she didn't judge. She always accepted us for who we were. When I was down and out, she still supported me and never abandoned me. She has always been there for me, and she always did whatever it took to make her family happy and love us the right way. With Daddy being so hard on her, we were all she had, and she put everything into raising us.

It may seem crazy to say that her love wasn't enough, but it still wasn't the same as having a real relationship with my father. The bond between fathers and daughters is special. It isn't like anything else in the world, and if you don't have it when you need it, you get confused, especially about men. If my daddy had been around, if he hadn't been in and out of jail, if he'd been someone I could really respect instead of someone who blew up about something as small as nail polish, I could have asked him for advice.

He knew a lot about the world and could have told me how to avoid guys who sleep around and try to talk down to women even when we're strong and independent. I would have been better at seeing through men with past issues they haven't worked on. If my daddy had been a real father to me, I would have stayed focused on my own life rather than looking for the love I was missing. I probably wouldn't have had a baby in my teens.

When he finally found out I was pregnant, he took an interest in me, because he wanted to control me. But by then, I was older and wise to his games. I will never forget the things he did to me and my mom, but it's right to forgive, and I do forgive him.

Not having my daddy as a loving, positive part of my life really affected how I thought about what I wanted for my own future kids. I didn't want to be a single mom. I never wanted a child of mine to grow up without a father, and I promised myself I would keep my family together no matter what, when the time came. I figured that would be a while yet—I was still in high school, after all. But life had other ideas, in the form of Terryl, whom I met right when my feelings of disappointment and anger about my daddy were at their most intense.

Terryl was irresistible to me. I was fifteen, and he told me he was sixteen. Oh, I wanted him, like all the girls did. He was gorgeous—so black, with pretty brown eyes that sparkled and laughed. He had an amazing sense of style, too. At first, we were just friends. I was messing around then with a guy from the hood, Tommy, who was light-skinned and sexy, but he was also a player and full of shit, so I broke up with him and fell hard for Terryl. He was the hottest thing I'd ever seen.

So Terryl and I got together. He was my Hershey bar, my love, my heart, my everything. He was the only thing that mattered to me, and I didn't care about or want to deal with anyone else. Looking back, I know I was obsessed with him. I wasn't going to let him go until I was ready, and in fact we were together on and off for almost ten years. I now know that was way too long for me to put up with his behavior, and that's part of why I'm writing this book—to help other women buy a clue and not stay in bad relationships for too long.

But at the beginning, I was in heaven. Time passed, and everything was cool. We shared so much. We talked about our feelings, but we also loved to crack jokes and play-fight. He was always sweet and respectful, and he didn't hide anything from me. He taught me so much. We went places together and stayed out late; he was always there, protecting me and treating me like a queen. At that time, sex wasn't on my mind, though probably he was thinking about it. But I was just focused on getting to know him and enjoying his company, because that's how I am. If I'm dealing with somebody, I go all out, and that's what I expect as well from those who respect me.

I didn't really know how to handle a relationship. I was just a young teenager, and my daddy wasn't at home to pick up on danger signals and warn me what Terryl was all about. My mom was around, but like most adolescents do, I'd reached a point in my life of thinking I knew it all and nobody could tell me anything. I was trying to figure it out for myself, and I hope my experiences can make things easier for someone else. It's true that love does crazy things to you, and I know it's not so easy to leave a partner when you're dangerously in love. It can be confusing, especially when you're young, to find the line between giving your all and putting up with too much.

I was trying to figure this out all on my own, and I was falling in love. I felt like I was more in love with him than he was with me, but I couldn't tell, because this was the first serious relationship I'd ever had. I hadn't experienced a broken heart, and I didn't have the skills to know what was real. He was a young, sexy black boy, and I didn't know what I was getting myself into. If I'd known, I would have stepped back a little.

However, I had to go through the pain, struggle, tears, fights, arguments, and much more. We had our ups and downs, but people saw us together so much that we were known all over town as Terryl and Asia. I thought we were in love, and that was the only thing that mattered. Now that I'm older, I know that "LOVE" is a big word. There's more to it than just saying it. You have to mean it with your actions. It's hard to live up to everything that word means, and now, you couldn't pay me enough to fall for that without seeing the actions that make it real and true.

As it was, Terryl gave me something I hadn't planned for: our beautiful daughter, born 6/15/2009. Nasia meant the world to me, and as I got more and more into being a mother, I realized I didn't care anymore whether my baby daddy was around, as long as I had my princess. Deep down inside, I knew I wasn't going to put up with his gaslighting and cheating. I'd rather be living life my way, on my terms, with my daughter. His cheating ways and messy traps weren't worth it.

I'm happy that I experienced the stuff I did, because sometimes life isn't all about you—it's about sharing what you've learned with others. Also, hard times help you to see who's really there for you. When you become a mom, everything changes. You have to become stronger and wiser and forget about what people say. You have to let go of worrying about people who don't approve of what you say and do. You have to just focus on getting through life and becoming a better person.

People come and go from your life every day. Your main focus should be yourself, putting God first, and being serious about your goals and responsibilities in life. Everything else comes second. If you don't figure that out, life can come crashing down on you, like it did for me when I realized I was pregnant.

Being pregnant at sixteen is already challenging, but on top of that, my princess was hard on my body. Luckily I was still living at home, and sometimes I stayed with my auntie, but I always had family support. I was glad I did, because I was still trying to finish school while being miserable during my pregnancy. I never got over being morning sick—it was more like all-day sick, and it lasted the whole nine months. My emotions were all over the place. I cried and fought with people; I felt lazy and couldn't eat even though I was big as a house.

At the same time, I loved having my princess in my belly and knowing she was with me all the time. She sure did a number on my tummy and the rest of my body, but even so, I loved her before I even met her. Terryl seemed to love her too, and that confused my heart even more. Even though he messed me over and made me cry so much that I felt I was losing my natural mind, he would talk to our baby and rub my big belly, and she would turn and kick for him. She even knew the sound of his voice, and I would feel her move when he was around. Those were some beautiful moments, when I knew his love for me and our baby was real. But he couldn't keep it up long enough for us to build a real life, and when you have a child, your priorities change. Suddenly, everything you were willing to handle before looks like something you want to run away from, to protect your baby.

I'd been with Terryl for five and a half years, but after Nasia was born, I knew I had to make a change. I started seeing a guy named Charlie, who took Terryl off my mind. We met during my last year of high school, and we became close friends. We weren't dating, but we did tell each other everything. He was funny and cool, and whenever I was down and out, he made me smile. I could always count on him to bring me up if I'd had a bad day. He was so different from Terryl. We were friends first; it wasn't just about the sex. But the sex was amazing—it was really making love, with both of us taking our time and treating each other right. I might never have had that experience if it hadn't been for my daughter, because becoming a mother woke me up to everything that was wrong in my life.

I took a long road to get to that realization, and I want to tell you some more about me and Terryl, because I know a lot of you reading this are in relationships that are bad like mine was, and if you see what I went through, I hope you'll make different and better choices than I did, rather than waiting and learning the hard way.

I know how you feel. When you've been to hell and back with somebody and shared a long-term relationship, you don't want to be with someone else or start the whole process all over again, trying to get to know someone new. It feels like you want to get a payoff for all the time you invested, so you stay steady and keep holding on. You figure that sooner or later, they'll be who you need them to be. But that's not how it works, and when you know, deep down, that the person you're with doesn't care about you the same way you care about them, you need to let go and stop paying that person any mind. You should be done with them!

Sometimes, it's good to look back at who you were and see how much you've changed. I'd like to share with you some of my diary entries from when things were bad. If any of this sounds familiar to you, then you're in a relationship you need to end.

7/11/2008: Thank you, God. It seems like a lot in my life has changed, in so many ways. I've really fallen in love with Terryl. We've been together for a while now, and it seemed so nice. But you know how girls want to get with him all the time, and it seems they want to mess up our relationship and what we've got going on. Every day, he tells me he loves me, but I don't know that's true just from him telling me. I have to see it for myself.

Whenever I'm with him, he makes me happy. I just want to know the truth about what goes on. I don't want him to hide anything from me, and I want to be honest with him. I feel like sometimes he doesn't know how good he has it, with a real woman who cares about him.

7/13/2008: I was chilling with Terryl tonight with a couple of friends, and after they left, I told him he was my heart, my everything. We even had sex, and he told me I was the first girl he'd ever had sex with. I didn't believe him, but the sex was so serious, and so good—I let him come in me. Afterwards, I don't remember exactly how it happened, but I confronted him with what I was hearing, that he's been talking to that one bitch, and he tried to brainwash me and tell me it was all in my head.

I just wanted the truth out of him, and I made him call her while I was sitting right there and tell her that he couldn't talk to or deal with her anymore. After that shit happened, my whole attitude changed, and we got into a big fight. He tried everything he could to make it up to me, even though I was so mad. I'm so stupid—I still love him, and I ain't gonna lie. L.O.V.E. is powerful!

7/17/2008: I lost it tonight with Terryl. I started going off, telling him, "Don't fuckin' play with me—stop acting like you don't give a fuck about me, 'cause I know where your heart is at."

I know that no matter what, I'm going to love him forever, regardless of the circumstances. I took a step back and heard out of his mouth that he doesn't care about me or love me. I know it's not true, but when your head is gone and you're stuck, you'll believe anything. I started crying in front of him, and he started pulling on me and trying to talk to me. He told me I was lucky and began to wipe my tears, but it didn't make any difference, because he was still gonna do what he does.

"How can you say I'm lucky?" I asked.

"'Cause I know what I did, and I know you're getting ready to be with me," he said. I told him no, I was getting ready to pull myself together and leave his ass. He wants me to believe that the way I act is what makes him cheat on me with those sluts, but from where I stand, if we're together, then we shouldn't be with anyone else. End of story.

7/19/2008: It's been two days since I saw Terryl. He keeps saying he's coming over, but he doesn't. I'm getting so mad at him, and I know that just makes him stay away. He hates it when I get mad because I can't control my anger, and I'm too quick to put my hands on him. I know I've gone too far sometimes. I've slapped him across the face, and once I even hit him with a hammer. I've burned his stuff, too. I know it's not right, but I can't help it. My anger is bigger than I am.

7/22/2008: Even when I'm sitting here by myself thinking about how much I care for Terryl, it kills me to know I love him too much. He knows he's got a good girl, and today turned out okay, but at the same time, it makes me mad to know I can talk all day to try to make him understand me, but I can't ever change how he feels. There's always some girl out there worrying about me and Terryl, wanting to break us up. It's none of their concern. Yes, things are hard, and I've fallen so far inside myself with anger and sadness that I don't even want to talk to anyone.

So I talked to him, and he gave me a real show, telling me how he'll be different and stop sleeping around. I'll believe it when I see it. Right now, I feel stuck and lost, and if I find out he's still cheating or sleeping around, I don't know what I'll do or say. I do know he can't hide from me forever, though, and if he fucks with me, I'll fuck with him. If he wants trouble, he'll get it.

I woke up after midnight, thinking about what he's said to me versus what he does. He told me he would be around, but he isn't. I see he does a lot to hurt me. He might mean well, but he doesn't follow through. I don't know what my next step is, so all I can do is ask God to make us stronger.

7/23/2008: On Thursday night I was sleeping and suddenly he called me, asking if we could be together, telling me he missed me and he's sorry. As usual, I was so caught up that I began to agree to take him back, just like always. Then he started up some crazy talk about "I hope we can get it together and stop all our bullshit," but I wasn't going to let that slide.

"I'm not fucking around on you," I said. "I don't want anyone else."

He said, "I can't let you go, and if you're trying to talk to someone else, you've got me all fucked up."

So we officially made up and we're together again, but I know he realizes he has it made, and he loves me too much to really let me go. I woke up from a long night and a crazy morning of talking to my sweetheart and then suddenly, I was in a lot of pain—terrible cramps, hurting so bad. I went into the bathroom and saw blood, but it was just spots. I didn't know if it was my period or if I was having a miscarriage. I heard someone say once that even if you're pregnant, you can still have a menstrual and see blood. I didn't know what to think, and I wasn't in the mood to worry about it.

I was glad we were back together, but I also felt defensive and scared. I didn't want him to touch, hug, or kiss me—I guess I was just being a little bitch, but after everything he put me through, I just wasn't in the mood. I told him not to come playing because he plays too much, and he needs to respect my privacy. When he's down and out, I don't play—I don't mess with him. He needs to understand that. I was worn out from it all and just wanted to rest.

7/24/2008: Terryl had to go, but every chance he got, he called and checked on me. He was trying to talk like a grown man, telling me how he loves me and how he is going to do right by me. He was crying and talking about how he has to get his shit together and act right. He said he doesn't want to leave me, and he doesn't want me talking to anyone else, but if he keeps doing like he does, that's how it's going to be. No matter what, I'll be here, but I really don't know what he wants to do with himself or where he wants to be. He should have learned his lesson by now.

We had a really intense time on Saturday. My cousin Naia and I were at my grandma's house, chilling with my homegirl Aimee, trying to find a ride so we could go see our boyfriends. I did everything I could to see Terryl, because he was my baby, and I would do anything for him. It was 11:00 by the time I finally got to him, but we made it, even though we were late.

Terryl and I were still mad at each other, but Naia and her boyfriend were all cuddled up. I left the living room and went to have a few minutes to myself and to get my head straight. I went into the bathroom to take a shower, and as I was coming out, Terryl came up to me and started kissing me. Even though we'd had a fight, we both knew our pattern already. We knew we'd make up.

I was kissing him back, and then we went to the bedroom and he laid me on the bed. He was on top of me and said he wanted to eat my pussy, but I didn't really want to do anything. I kept telling myself over and over again, *We're not gonna have sex. We're not gonna have sex.* But I fell for it anyway. Somehow, some way—I can't lie; it got so real, and the sex got crazy. At one point, I was even sucking his dick, which I shouldn't have done because he didn't deserve it. But there we were, and I was pulling his clothes off.

We went back to the bathroom and I started running the water so we could take a shower together. We were making love in the shower and I asked him, "Do you want to fuck me from behind?"

He said, "Hell yeah" and bent me over. I was screaming and making all types of sounds. He stuck his dick in me like he never did before—it hurt so bad. But I took it. First I was holding on to the sink, then the tub, then I was holding my ankles. This was shit I never did before. Afterward, he seemed to know he'd gone too far.

"Baby, I'm sorry," he said, and we cuddled up together. He told me about everything he wants from life—how he wants me to have his baby so we can be a real family.

That sounds too good to be true. But I can't lie—he means the world to me.

8/28/2008: It's the same old thing. I'm still with Terryl. He was kissing on me all morning, and sometimes when I'm with him, he makes me happy and I enjoy my time with him. Then, all of a sudden, I saw patchy marks on my neck. He said, "Baby, I had to do it," and then he was kissing my stomach.

He can be so sweet. Today was the first time we'd seen each other in a few days—as usual, I was out waiting for his call, but I tried to keep it together. Today I went to his house, and then he and I went to my auntie's house and he spent the night with me. Yes, that's my baby, and I love him so much. Sure, he makes me sick sometimes, but that's the price of being with him.

Today we made love and had fun and saw his family. I know there are people who don't want us to be happy, especially the other girls that want to get with him. But no matter what, I'll be by his side.

8/29/2008: It's another day, and I already know I don't want to be messing around. I know I won't have sex with my boyfriend today. It's not a good time—my damn pussy is in pain from the other nights we had sex. It's so small and tight, not loose and out of control. And now I'm home alone missing him, and he has my phone, so I'm bored now.

But for a while, he's been here spending quality time with me and my family.

We fucked all night long, so many times, and of course he came in me, and he even ate me out. He told me that he loves me and doesn't want to let me go, but even after all that, I still don't trust him. I think he'll end up doing dumb shit again. It's not about the sex, though I hate the idea of him sleeping with anyone else. It's more about respect and what we have going on.

After the sun went down, we went to the park and we were walking and talking. We started to argue, and it was like I blacked out—I got so mad, and we got into it. I hit him, and he hit me back. Then I punched him in the nose and he started bleeding. He called me out for my attitude and I didn't want to talk about it, so I left it at that.

We went back home, and later when we were watching TV, he started to touch and kiss me. I couldn't stay mad at him. I'd been thinking about how much fun we've had together—double dating with our friends, going to movies, just chilling and talking to each other. When things are good, he makes me so happy. I started coming on to him. I got on top of him, riding him, bouncing on his dick. I came so hard on his dick. We went all night and did everything—we made love and ended by talking, sharing time, discussing our problems.

One of our problems is his family. His friends hate me and his mama is a crazy bitch who doesn't want him to be with me. Even his fat-ass sister is a bitch to me. Every chance she gets, she starts acting crazy. The more those bitches don't want me around, the more I show up. It doesn't matter what they think—I'm not sleeping with them or dating them, so why should they care? I'm not in it for them. I'm in it for Terryl. I care for him, and more than that, I love him. It's not something I can get out of, even if I wanted to.

I think they don't like me because I have a mind of my own. I'm outspoken and I don't care what comes out of my mouth. He's used to being spoiled like a little boy. They let him do anything he wants instead of teaching him the right stuff. But that's not doing him any good—he needs to be a man and grow up. I'm giving him the chance to do that, and those bitches don't like it.

I know I'm lucky to have grown up in a house where I have everything I need. Terryl's family is really poor. They can't even pay their gas bill, so they can't cook on the stove or use their water heater. They have to warm up water in the microwave to take a bath or wash. Terryl's mom gets high and spends money on drugs instead of on bills. But I don't care about any of that because I love him for who he is. I see other things in him, though, and I feel like he's happier when he's with me, at my house or my auntie's house. I think he feels more comfortable at my auntie's, because her hood is more ghetto, more what he's used to.

I want him to be with me and have the lifestyle I grew up with. There's nothing wrong with being poor—you have to crawl before you can walk—and in order to have more you have to want it and do better. I just want him to see what's possible for him, even if that pisses off his family.

9/3/2008: Nothing too major today. Terryl came over and we sat and talked. He was kissing me and making me laugh. I love to be with him when he's like this. He's so funny, and he looks so freaking good. But then he hung out with his friends for a while, and he started talking about some girls. I didn't want to hear that shit, so I left. He was mad, but oh well. It seems like every time we get back on track, he goes off again. We go through so many cycles of breaking up and making up that it's starting to get old. In different ways, it seems like he's starting to show me that he doesn't want to be with me. It hurts to know that I love him, but he's still acting out this bullshit.

9/4/2008: I haven't been myself for the last couple of days, and

Terryl has been acting stupid and not coming around. I'm going to talk to him and see what he says and get some help soon, because I can't take this too much longer. We haven't had sex for a couple of days, but I don't care. It's the same old shit.

I got dressed and pulled myself together today to go out, feel the breeze, and see what was popping. I saw him with that black bitch he said he wouldn't see any more. I saw with my own eyes that he's still lying. He keeps saying he loves me, but I don't know how much longer I can take knowing that he's cheating on me. I think it's best for me to be nasty and beat him at his own game. Yeah, it's messed up, but I'm gonna fix him, good—I may be hurting, but I know how to hurt him back, and I will. I'm starting to hate his ass. I'm heartbroken.

9/5/2008: It's Friday night, and although I was trying to sleep, something just kept distracting me. I guess I was too busy being stuck on him, missing him so much that I couldn't sleep. I missed his touch, his kisses, his smile, and much, much more. I was just thinking and thinking about him. He came over to talk to my older cousin, and then he began that lying shit, telling me how much he missed me. "Whatever, guy—stop the bullshit and keep it moving," I wanted to say.

9/7/2008: Terryl was over here spouting his same old shit. "You're my baby, and even if we do break up, I'm going to be fucking you sometimes. I love you, girl, like a fat boy loves cheeseburgers. You are my honey buns, my sweetheart, my cupcake. I swear, you want me to beat your ass, but I can't hit you. You make me smile. I will never find another girl like you, for real."

I know he meant it, because of the stuff he does and the way he acts—he won't get in trouble for another bitch, but he will for me. After he went home and I was trying to get some sleep, he called and told me that his mama was going nuts on him. She got on the phone, talking crazy, saying he couldn't stay overnight with me or come over anymore. I don't know why she's trying to pull that game now. I am going to be with him no matter what. I love him, and if he has to leave home and stay with me instead, then that's what will happen.

I told his mama that I might be pregnant, and she went crazy when I said it. I guess she's afraid that I'll ask for child support, but I wouldn't do anything to hurt Terryl. Then she told me she would call the police on me. Even here in my diary, it's painful to say why. Terryl is only thirteen. I thought he was at least fifteen. But I'm three years older than he is, and his mama and sister have accused me of rape, which is ridiculous. Terryl may be young, but all anyone has to do is look at his cheating ways to know there wasn't any rape involved here with me or any of those other girls he's been with.

His mama, sister, and anyone else who has something to say can kiss my ass. What we have is between me and Terryl, and nobody else should be up in our business.

9/8/2008: I'm having a good day so far. I saw Terryl, and we talked about the fact that I think he's been sleeping around with this girl Amanda. He keeps telling me I'm just tripping, and she's just a friend. I want to know whether he really loves me. I know he's got other problems right now, though. His mama is acting stupid—she kicked Terryl out of the house. He's so mad, he couldn't even go to football practice. She thinks I called Terryl's daddy to talk shit about her, and so now I have to worry about that. But the good part is that since she kicked him out, Terryl is staying with me, and we made love again and again, all night long.

9/9/2008: Nothing much going on. I got Terryl cleaned up and walked him to the bus stop this morning. She keeps calling, but she also still wants him out of her house. She can't have it both ways. He's been away from home for four days now, and we're getting on really well. It's funny, he's worried about guys chasing after me, but he doesn't like it when I tell him not to mess with me and hang with other girls. He's like his mama—he wants it both ways. Well, neither of them can have what they want. It's one way or the other; that's how it works.

9/10/2008: I was with Terryl and he ended up being late for school. I wanted to go to school today, but something was wrong with me—I don't know what, but I just hurt all over and didn't want to deal with anybody. When I woke up, I learned that now Terryl's daddy doesn't want him to be with me, either. Between his family and the girls who want to get with him, it's hard sometimes to stay hopeful. But we're going to be together no matter what anyone thinks.

9/11/2008: I'm just praying today about everything that Terryl and I are going through. I'm even praying for his daddy and mama, even though they hate me. I pray that they'll see how good I am for Terryl and how much I love him. But even if they don't, he's going to be with me no matter what.

His daddy threw my phone on the ground and cracked the screen—such a nasty thing to do, but still I want God to forgive my sins and bless them. I know everything will work out. Lord, just watch me! I hope to go to church this weekend.

9/12/2008: Maybe I don't really know what love is, but I think I love Terryl. I've been thinking a lot about what happened when his daddy broke my phone. Terryl was so mad. He said, "I hate that guy. He ain't gonna break me and you up." When his daddy wrecked my phone, Terryl pushed him! He actually chose me over his daddy, so I know he really loves me. "I guess I'm gonna have to start hustling for

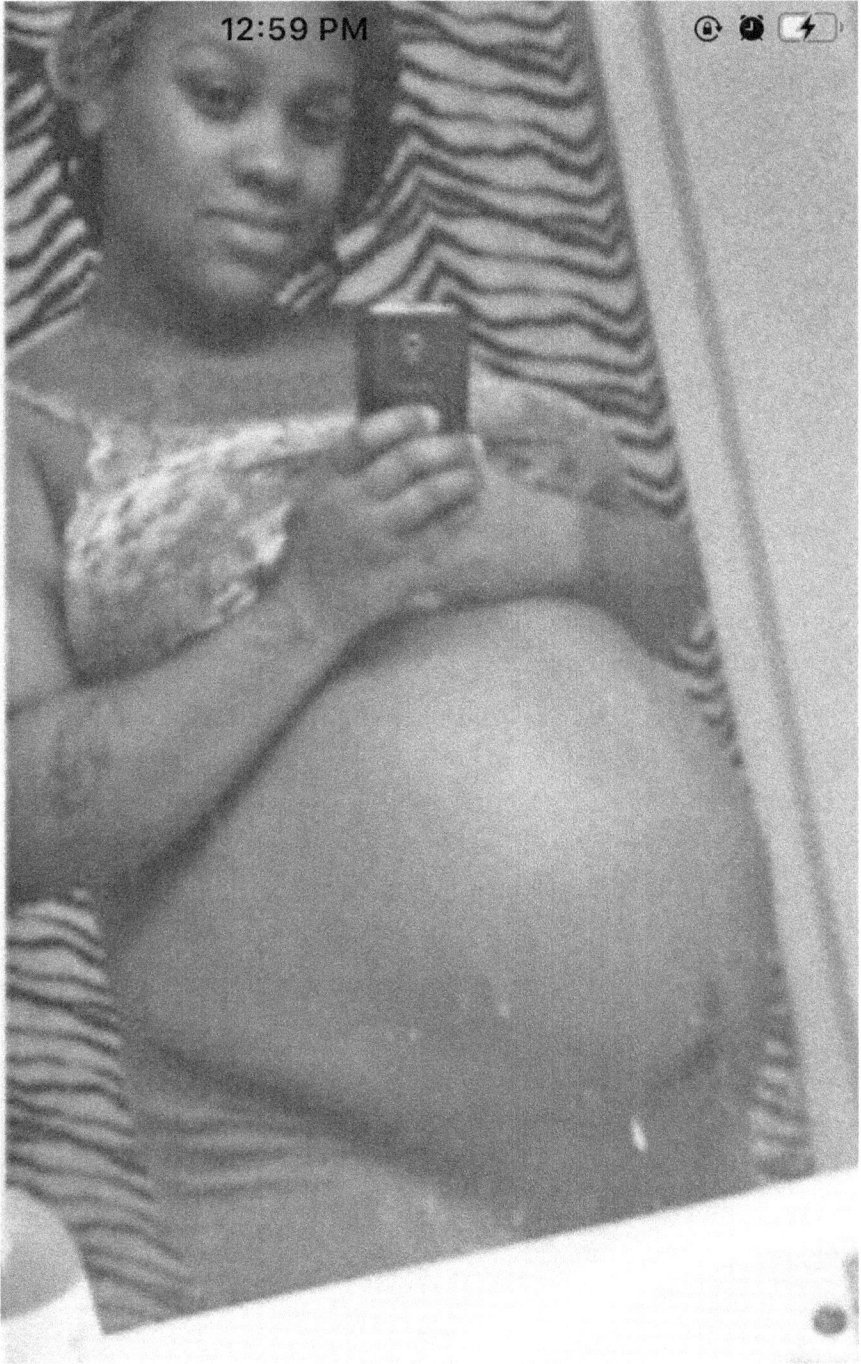

you, baby," Terryl told me.

Some bitches think he's going to leave me, but the joke's on them. Lately we've been hanging at my auntie's house. Her neighborhood is more ghetto, but that's okay with us. We were hanging out and having fun. I loved staying there, and Terryl likes being at her place. His mama won't let me go to their house, and she doesn't want him spending time with me. It's harder to find us at my auntie's house. I'm not saying my mama doesn't care what I do, but she's not much use to us in this situation or really aware yet of what's going on.

Terryl and I made love all night, so many times, till it didn't even make sense. I love him so much.

9/13/2008: Tonight I'm sitting with my baby and thinking about how sick I am of all the shit from his family. It's crazy but also kind of funny. His mama called looking for him, but he was with me and didn't want to talk to her.

I don't understand the stuff she's doing. It's really hurting him, and he never really got into anything bad until they started the drama. His mama lets him deal drugs from her house and never says anything about it. The bad shit he's into has nothing to do with me—I'm a good influence on him. But his mama would rather have him under her control, even if it's bad for him. She just doesn't really care.

Also, I'm starting to wonder if I may be pregnant. Terryl and I have talked about that a lot, and I know he wants to start a family with me.

"Baby, I can't resist you," he said to me. "My mama is trying to make me stop being with you, but I'm in love with you for real, and if I leave, it will hurt me too much. I hope you really are pregnant, so they can have something to talk about! Just know that no matter what, I'm still gonna be there forever."

9/15/2008: Today I didn't do anything except see Terryl. Yes, he's been over here again, and he always tells me what the other girls are saying, 'cause they're always talking about some shit. They think they know everything. But anyway, I love him, and that's me. No matter what those bitches say, I'm just me, and I'll stay real and let their criticism roll off my back. I don't need to pay attention to what they say. Terryl and I made love earlier and it was good—and that's all I need.

9/17/2008: I'm just chilling. People are still mad that we are together. Today Terryl said to me, "I'm gonna beat your ass for real if you don't stop smoking. If you think you might be having my baby and you do anything to hurt it, I'm gonna be mad even though I love you."

I know he wouldn't ever really hurt me, but it makes me feel good that he cares so much about what might happen to me and our baby, if I really am pregnant. I think I am, because I'm getting fatter, and I've never had a problem with my weight. My stomach suddenly looks swollen up. I really noticed it when I got out of the shower today, after Terryl and I made love. My periods have always been unpredictable, so I'm not sure. But I think it's for real this time.

9/18/2008: Man, it seems like the closer we get, the more people start acting crazy about us being together. His horrible mama even came around here looking for him. She started talking crazy about filing a rape charge against me because Terryl is younger than I am.

"You crazy bitch—you sound stupid as fuck," I told her.

Anyway, if I'm carrying his baby, she's going to be really mad and hate me even more. But no matter what, I'm going to be with Terryl. And if she starts threatening me again with the police—well, maybe she's forgetting that I know about the drug deals happening in her very own house, which she allows. If she messes with me, she'll regret it. I know she doesn't want me to say anything about the drugs. I'm so sick of her shit.

9/19/2008: So I guess Terryl's mama called my mama today. She's got some real nerve, but I really don't care. Terryl told his mama that I'm pregnant, and his mama asked my mama about it, and my mama asked me, and I said I don't know for sure. I should probably go to the drugstore and get a pregnancy test, but some part of me doesn't really want to know. I mean, if I'm not pregnant, then I'm just getting fat, and I don't want to deal with that. And I know Terryl would be disappointed, and I don't want to do that to him.

If I really am pregnant, we'll know pretty soon. Also, if I know for sure I'm pregnant, shit is going down with his family for real, and I don't want to deal with it. I'm so sick of it. Terryl's mama pretends and is always been fake. She says I'm not trustworthy and says if I'm pregnant, she's going to get a blood test to prove it's not Terryl's. But guess what? I haven't been with anyone else, no matter what she thinks.

Fuck everybody. I mean that. Fuck Terryl's mama and daddy, his whole family, the people all up in my business, and everyone else who doesn't want me and Terryl together, just talking about me like they know me.

9/20/2008: I saw Terryl today and couldn't stop crying because everything is so out of control. People need to stop worrying about me and worry about themselves. Terryl and I are good together. Why can't we just be happy together, without his family and all these random girls trying to break us up?

9/22/2008: Bright and early in the morning, Terryl came over and was playing and stuff. Now, people are threatening to tell him that I was smoking. Damn—worry about yourselves! Lately he hasn't been spending the night because of the issues with his people, and he says I have to get used to it.

9/23/2008: Terryl was over today, acting like he's not in his right mind. It seems like there's something wrong with him. I know he'll tell me about it sooner or later, so for now I'm going to keep to myself and give him space. But this Friday, we're supposed to go to the doctor for a regular check-up.

9/24/2008: This just isn't my day. Terryl is always trying to find out shit about me. I'm sick of arguing with him and playing games, so now is the time to stop all this. I'm tired of all this little-boy drama. I deserve a grown-ass man who will help me and our baby and who wants to be in our life.

I told Terryl, "It isn't worth it, me looking good on the outside but hurting inside. All the times I've been there for your black ass, and all you do is cheat. I know about that girl Jasmine you've been chasing, and I know that after you think about things, you'll be back again like you always are. You know I've done right by you. Cry if you want, but it doesn't mean anything. Either you're going to change for real, or you're not."

I can't give in. I have to be strong.

10/23/2008: I'm wondering why I keep putting myself in this predicament. It's like Terryl thinks I'm never going to catch on, like I don't know anything. But I figure stuff out real fast. I'm still feeling sick, and I have a lot on my mind. I'm trying to trust in the Lord and focus on prayer.

10/24/2008: I don't have anything to do today, so I guess I'll go to my auntie's house and hang out. Somehow, every time I decide to stop worrying about Terryl, he starts to pop up out of nowhere. My hormones are starting to mess with me, and I was crying and crying. Terryl showed up and tried to talk to me. I asked him how he feels about me, and he said he loves me and hated to see us doing badly together. He said he loves it when we're together, and he knows he's messed up, and he doesn't want to let me go.

I've heard that too many times already. I was so mad all night—I was acting crazy.

10/29/2008: God is always a blessing. When bad things happen, I can always remind myself that I am already covered in the blood of Jesus. I've been spending a lot of time in prayer and focusing on what's in my mind and heart. I said to myself, "If I leave Terryl, he's not going to know what to do. Why not leave him and find someone who treats me right? If it's meant to be, we will still be together. It's time to move on, and it's time to just do me. I won't call him, and he won't have to call me."

He said he would be around and support me during my pregnancy, and he's not being true to his word. Being honest and living up to what you say you'll do is all that really matters I life. It's messed up the way guys do females and how they leave them. I've got to have faith that I can just do what I need to do. I'm asking myself these questions:

1. If I leave him, would he ever come back?
2. Why does he do the awful things he does to me?
3. Does he do these things just to hurt me, or is it that he can't help it?
4. Will he ever be with me and our baby?
5. How do I stop being in love with him?
6. Would my life be better without him?

I can't answer any of these questions, so I have to give them to God and trust that He will make a way for me.

ASIA CARRACTER

10/30/2008: I feel so good today and feel like I don't need Terryl, but I know I'm still dangerously in love with him. I'm doing great without him right now, though. If he wants to sleep around, then let him. I'm going to show him what he's lost. He already knows, but I want him to really feel it. I know God will make a way.

10/31/2008: It's a new day for me. I told myself that I have to stand up for what I want and tell Terryl that I'm not going to keep taking him back. I am doing fine without him. I'm not crying or stressing out all the time like I was when we were together. I know he's already missing me because he told Matt, and Matt told me. Matt said that Terryl asked him to call me to see if I'm okay. I told Matt I'm fine.

I'm three months pregnant, and I haven't seen or talked to Terryl at all for more than a week. I really miss him, but already I see a difference in my life, without all the drama. This all has to stop, and I have to better myself. In my heart, I know that nothing will change in my life as long as I'm with him.

11/1/2008: I pray constantly, and I know that God is good. Thank you, Lord, for waking me up to what I need in my life. I'm in the third month of my pregnancy and doing okay.

11/2/2008: I'm becoming so much stronger. Terryl's mama and I have had our ups and downs, but now that Terryl and I haven't seen each other in a while, his mama seems a lot nicer. It may seem crazy that I'm talking to her, but she's the one who can really help me to understand what's going on with him. She says he's acting crazy and claiming that my baby isn't his, when he knows perfectly well it is. But I'm going to do me and not worry about what he thinks.

When you end up pregnant, that's when a guy will try to run game on you and act funny and try to dis your baby, when he knows you were faithful to him and it's his child. His mama told me, "That's how guys do." She knows how it is, and now that Terryl is doing me wrong, she seems to understand me a lot better and wants to be my friend.

I'm going to keep talking to her and let her know what's going on with the baby. She will see that I'm a good person and that all the drama she and I had was about Terryl. I'm glad she's willing to talk to me. I never expected anything from her. It just goes to show—you never know.

11/7/2008: Terryl called a couple nights ago, finally, but I don't want anything to do with him. I'm good without him—so much better, actually. I'm still talking to his mama, and that still feels good. I'm spending a lot of time with family and friends. Today I'm getting my hustle on to try to figure out how to get some money. I'm going to need a real job to take care of my baby when she comes, but in the meantime, I can do hair and other things.

11/9/2008: I talked to Terryl's mama today and she told me some girls were playing on her phone. Even though she's been a lot nicer to me lately, it's hard for me to have respect for her because she wants to blame other people for the shit she allows. She lets Terryl sell drugs out of her house and bring girls to her home to sleep with in her house. She let him grow up to be who he is and didn't give him any guidance or teach him the difference between right and wrong.

I keep realizing how different his family is from mine. Terryl and I would talk about making big plans, having a family, starting a business, I didn't know what the next step would be for him—it was all just a fantasy. He doesn't have what it takes to do the right thing because he's never seen anyone doing the right thing.

I think he wanted to be with me partly because I have what it takes, and he knows that, and he wants a better life. But as long as his family keeps letting him do what he does, he'll never have a reason to change. I can't forget how hurtful Terryl's family was to me and how his mama wanted to accuse me of all these things going on, even though it wasn't my fault that he lied about his age. I guess it was just too hard for them to accept that this young boy had a baby on the way. I wish I'd been stronger earlier in our relationship and walked away from the spiteful things they were saying. I wish I'd walked away from him fast enough. But it is what it is, and now I'm going to do the best I can with what I have, with God's help.

11/17/2008: Pretty quiet the past few days. I went to the doctor and he checked on the baby and gave me some vitamin pills to take. I thank the Lord I'm healthy. I don't really want to do anything but sleep.

11/15/2008: I went to the doctor again today to get my shots, and I heard my baby's heartbeat for the first time. I can't believe I'm already fifteen weeks along. The rest of the day, I've been chilling with my cousin. I feel so much better away from Terryl. I'm hearing from some of our friends that he wants to do right by me, but I don't trust him. I'm better off on my own, with my family.

11/24/2008: The same bitches as usual started playing with me on my phone, talking crazy about my baby, saying she would be ugly and they hoped something would happen to me and her, but I don't care anymore. They can have Terryl. I don't have to worry anymore. I'm focused on my life and my child. I'm becoming stronger and handling my business. I have a child coming into this world, and there's nothing more important than that.

The bigger my stomach gets, the more I stop worrying about my baby's father. Don't get me wrong—I loved him, and he hurt me. But's best to play the cards you're dealt and stop trying to force things to be different. I never would have thought I could go through so much, but I've learned from my mistakes.

As you can see from reading my diary, separating from Terryl wasn't easy, but being pregnant really inspired me to try to get myself together. I have to be honest and tell you that once I started showing closer to my due date, I let him come around sometimes. I had friends, but I never slept with them, and I'd rather have sex with my child's father than with somebody I don't know. We had so much history—it was hard to say goodbye completely. But I was tired of hurting and crying, and things weren't the way they used to be with Terryl. I wasn't putting up with his shit in the same way.

Terryl seemed to want to be part of his baby's life, but I was determined to be as independent as possible so he couldn't keep messing with me. For our baby's sake, I wanted to be stable, and that didn't include drama with Terryl and his lying-ass ways.

For some reason, his family was convinced that I was having a boy, but when I found out I was having a girl, Terryl was so happy. He said he'd always hoped we would have a daughter. It was hard not to get caught up with him in dreams that could never come true. He still thought we could make a real life together, even though he didn't have what it takes. I tried to let him down easy, though.

Together we decided to name our daughter Nasia—it's a beautiful name that nobody else has. We love the name, and I know we both love her, even though he's not able to show up for her the way a daddy should.

I gave my life over to God, and I felt good about that. Life still had some surprises waiting for me, though.

I'd known Big J for a long time. We went to school together, and we would talk on the phone. Sometimes he'd come over with his brother Tim after school, and we would hang out. At first, I thought I wasn't interested in being with him, but as time passed, we got closer and closer. We were comfortable with each other. He knew all about my past, so I didn't have to explain everything to him all the time. We shared stories and helped each other with our problems.

But then, all of a sudden, I stopped seeing him and his brother around the neighborhood. I found out that they got picked up on an old drug charge and had to do three months in jail. I wrote to him, asking questions about his case. He never lied to me, and we kept it real. That has been so rare in my life—men who keep it real and tell the truth. I respected him because he let me know what the deal was.

Even though I kept telling him I just wanted to be friends because I was so stuck on Terryl, Big J told me I was too good to be treated the way Terryl did me. Our friendship got so deep that I could tell him anything. Every time I talked to him, he made me smile. We were a lot alike—we loved to play and crack jokes. And we were both Tauruses, so we got along really well. He always told me how much he cared about me. I couldn't ever lie to him. I didn't have to be fake or do anything other than be completely myself with him. I felt like I was learning more about myself, seeing things differently.

After I got some distance from Terryl, I realized I really liked Big J. It was hard, because of all I'd been through. It was hard to trust that J wouldn't pull the same shit that Terryl had always put me through. Some days I'd wake up feeling angry or defensive even though nothing had happened and J had done nothing to hurt me.

It's hard not to hold on to the past, and I know from experience that sometimes when things are better, all you can do is cry from relief.

Looking back in my diary, I wrote this about being with J: "I am having a good friendship. Every time I wake up, I thank God. I am so blessed. Every time I look at myself, I ask myself where I would be if it wasn't for J. Now I'm happy, and I don't have to cry any more. The old things I used to do are over. I don't have to be fucked up with Terryl. I'm happy that I'm free, and I can't go backwards. My heart is filled with someone who cares about me."

I got out of jail, and not long after, he died. He called me the night he died, and I didn't take his call. When I heard what happened, I thought I was going crazy, or that it was a dream. I was losing my mind, thinking it couldn't be true. Why didn't I talk to him? Why did this happen to him? All I could say to the people calling me was, "I don't believe he's gone."

There's no pain like knowing that the person you shared time with is gone so fast. We spent so much time together and shared so much—and he had just gotten out of jail, ready to start his new life. I still don't know all the details of what happened or why, just that he was shot and killed. I never imagined that he would be gone, but at the same time, looking back, I should have anticipated that some tragedy would happen, if I'd put together the pieces of what he told me—but I never did.

His family and I still miss him every day. His death really hurt his family, too—they were really close, the kind of family that loved to do everything together and kept close. He's still in my heart, and everyone who knew him remembers him with love. He died on December 15th, so the holidays are hard for everyone who knew him. I'll never forget him, and I still have all the letters he wrote to me.

It was hard to go on after that. I was still trying to find myself, and afterward I ended up back with Terryl for a while. I felt so alone, and he wanted to be involved with his daughter. It seemed like maybe he was trying to straighten himself out. Even though we were just teenagers, not knowing what we were doing, we'd done a lot of talking about how we wanted our lives to be. I still think that deep down, the best parts of who he was really meant what he said about wanting to be a family, and at that time, I was vulnerable to him. I felt I owed him another chance, and I owed Nasia a chance to know her daddy.

Terryl and I got pregnant again, and in 2014, we had our baby boy. When we had our second child, a son, I thought Terryl would be better, and that this time he would really change, like he kept promising to do. But he still couldn't get himself together. I realized this time I had to let him go for real, before my rage and frustration caused me to do something violent toward him. The weeks right after I had my baby boy really showed me that I needed to let Terryl go. He was treating me horribly and cheating on me, and his mama was allowing him to sleep with other girls under her roof when my baby wasn't even three weeks old.

I was at home taking care of our children, and he was at his mama's house with another woman and her kids, who were sleeping on his mama's sofa. One day, I dropped by Terryl's mama's house with the kids because he wasn't answering the phone and I was worried. Before I could even get in the door, Terryl's little niece said to me, "Terryl's got a girl here."

I've never felt so angry in my life. I thought I'd known before that I needed to get rid of him, but this time, I knew it in every cell of my body. I went crazy—I couldn't control myself. I rushed into the house, pulled out my pepper spray, and hit Terryl in the face with it, looking for the girl he had there.

"You can't play around with me—I'll show you!" I yelled. I took both of his phones—one was the phone we talked on, and the other was the one he used for his drug deals. I broke both of them and cut off his phone service, and when I got home, I didn't even cry. I just ended up burning the clothes he had at my place.

He didn't care about anyone or anything—he was just sleeping around and endangering me and the kids. He ended up catching an STD. His mom called to tell me about it, and I said, "God was looking out for me. I haven't been sleeping with him, and he's picking up diseases from these nasty girls."

He always looked so sweet on the outside, but after what I'd seen and what I knew, I had to go. It hurt like crazy and wasn't easy, because we'd been together for ten years on and off. He was doing things I couldn't overlook or forgive—the same old shit, chasing pussy, sleeping around, not being there for me or the kids. I ended up cutting him out of my life entirely because he wasn't being a father to his children anyway. He talked big about wanting to be a family, he rarely saw or even asked about the kids, and he never attended school events. He didn't show up when the kids or I needed a ride. He broke promise after promise, time after time. He was just a failure.

After the birth of our second child, the system caught up with him and demanded that he pay child support. He couldn't pay it for Nasia because he was young and living with his mother, so it had to wait until he was older and got a job. The child support was a lot less important to me than my kids having a real father in their lives. That was what they needed the most.

Terryl broke me down so bad that I thought I wouldn't ever be able to love again. He played mind games and told me that nobody would want a woman who had two kids and that nobody else would ever love me. Let's be real and honest—for a while, I believed him. My beliefs began to change when I began to hold myself accountable for my decisions and actions and for the things I have allowed.

I was a woman now, not a teenager anymore. I had to sit down and analyze myself. I stayed believing he would change, despite every piece of evidence to the contrary. Eventually, I had to step back and let him do his own thing, rather than trying to control him. He was a little boy when we met, and even after he grew up, he was still like a little boy. There's no way I can make a man step up and change. He was still growing up and didn't know himself.

I learned that the only person I can control is myself, and it was time for me to grow up and let him find his own path. He really was too young to be a father, and if I'd understood that sooner, I probably

ASIA CARRACTER

would have made different decisions. I kept thinking that if I did the right thing, he would do the right thing, too. I took him in when nobody wanted him; I fed him when he was hungry, comforted him when he was hurting. My family and I were good to him, and I kept seeing glimpses of the real Terryl. But he wasn't ready to be a man. He needed to put his childish ways aside, but he couldn't get there, and I wasted ten years on nothing.

It took me a while to come back from that. I was completely broken in so many ways, and every time I looked around, I would say to myself, "Men ain't shit," all because one guy messed me over. I didn't want to love again. I just wanted to sleep around and have fun, which I did because I was hurt. I never really talked to people about what was going on with me. It was just a type of feeling I couldn't even explain, like I had no heart.

At the same time, my mind was messed up because of the unbearable pain of looking at men and knowing I didn't care about them as people—I just wanted them to get laid and for what they could do for me. I got whatever I wanted. I was offered dates with all kinds of men, from sugar daddies to hot younger guys. But even while I was having sex with other guys, I was still thinking about Terryl. I would go to bed with a guy and keep him moving along with no emotional attachment …that's where I was. I was bitter, knowing that Terryl had hurt me so deeply, cheated on me so many times, and cared so little about my feelings.

I really wanted to talk to someone who would understand how I felt, but somehow, I couldn't. I just started doing whatever I could to heal, and part of healing was waking up to the fact that what I was doing didn't make sense. I'd have sex with a guy and then send him home, not caring how he felt about me. Then, I would cry and cry. I knew I had to stop acting like this sooner or later before I got hurt or one of these guys developed real feelings for me. If I felt like a guy felt something real for me, I'd cut him off and ignore him. I was trying to mend the broken spot and fill the hole of loneliness inside me.

Finally, I wanted to change. I wanted healing, and I wanted love. I wanted to be a different woman with a supportive partner, a stable man, a provider who would help me and my kids to live. I knew I couldn't have those things if I kept acting the way I was, not letting anyone get close to me. I had to change and heal those wounded feelings.

One day, things began to change. I ended up getting into a bad car accident, and life got rocky. It took a long time for me to get over my injuries from the accident, and I spent three years not dating anyone, just focusing on healing my body and my eyesight, which were damaged in the crash. That's how I healed and changed—I spent time alone and prayed, and when I came out of it, I began to know who I was and what I was worth.

I want to finish this book by giving some general advice that I've learned from my life experience. I can tell you that it's not all about a guy, it's all about yourself. I have learned that I can no longer worry about other people's problems—it's much easier said than done, I know, but when you've got yourself and have a broader perspective, things are clearer.

Sometimes you really do need just one person who may understand you, and it's important to know who your real friends are. A real friend stays by your side and never acts funny with you. They enjoy who you are, cry with you, and deal with you even when things are hard. As you go through life, you find out more and more, but you should still be focused on yourself first.

Once you put your mind to it and just think about yourself, you'll see where other people are making life harder for you. You need to be down for yourself and the few people who really want to deal with you—the ones who keep it real even when you're not around, rather than just saying the right things to your face.

I'm sharing my story because I know a lot of people are going through the same kinds of things I did. I love to influence people, encourage them, and give good advice. I know now that I won't settle for less than I deserve. Being in an abusive relationship is something I won't tolerate. I will not let a guy beat on me or talk to me like shit. I hate when guys do that and think it's cute. Some of these guys will even try to run game and talk to you like trash. You shouldn't let anybody control you or put up with things that aren't making you happy. I know there may be a lot of young girls in similar situations. It isn't always men who make women miserable, but I feel like women go through the most with the men in their lives, but life itself goes on, and you have to play the cards you're dealt. If you put up with too much, you can end up like me, making the wrong choices.

I love my life enough not to go through things I shouldn't be dealing with now. I am proud of myself in these joyful days. I'm so happy that I'm not stressed and crying or going through the foolishness and stupidity I went through with Terryl. I'd rather be alone than dealing with that. Let me tell you, a guy will do anything to you that you'll allow—trust me on that. It's okay for you to make mistakes, but it doesn't make sense to keep making the same mistake again and again. When you've already been down that road, you know where it leads. Turn the other way and try another road.

I chose a different road myself, and I'm both wiser and smarter now. I have created different standards, and I don't worry, thanks to my Father the Lord God. I want people to know that you don't have to deal with that shit you're going through. Keep God first and stay strong. He will be by your side. Give Him all your problems and whatever you're going through. Just keep praying, and I promise, everything will be better.

Sometimes in life, it's better to let go of what you think you want, because it's not worth your time and there is too much crap involved. I tell myself all the time that I'm thankful. In life, it takes time to let go, but it's always a lesson learned! No one deserves to be in a relationship with someone who doesn't want you to be happy or who always wants to keep you down. You have to be true to yourself and make your life better for you.

It's so crazy what love can do to you. It can mess up your head in so many ways. I just don't see myself putting up with that situation ever again. I'm better than any of that, and I'd rather be by myself. Love isn't worth shit unless it's real, and these guys don't seem to know what real is.

When I was going through the worst times, I never thought I'd be writing about my personal life. It's so crazy. I remember there was a time when I used to just sit there and cry, questioning myself. It's hard, when your back is against the wall and you're not really sharing your thoughts with anybody. It's like you have a million people sitting around just judging you, not even knowing what is going on with you, and at the end of the day, you have your own back. I've seen this so many times.

But when you learn better, you get to tell different people about your life and you begin to help others, even when it's hard. I always give straight talk to my friends and other people, to help them live a better life than I did as an adolescent. I love the fact that I have a real mother and an amazing grandmother, even though my grandmother would complain about every little thing. I understand why she did that—she wanted her grandkids to be good people and help her just like she helped us.

I love my family, and I don't know where I'd be without them. They've kept me going. My family have been my real parents, not like some. I love my family the most—thank you, Lord, for my precious family, especially my mama, who was always available with advice and help. What would I do without them? They're such a big help to me, always. They stuck with me when I was in love and going through bullshit, crying in pain. I also had a few close friends who helped me out just like family, and I will always be grateful to them. I can see this a lot more clearly now that I'm not in a toxic relationship.

As of this writing, I'm engaged to a man who has a real relationship with me and my kids. When I think of where I used to be and where I am now, I look around and I see people in love doing dumb stuff and being fools just like me. It hurts me to bad to see it. As you get older and wiser, you start asking yourself questions, particularly why women put up with abusive, controlling relationships. I want to tell you all that you shouldn't deal with or endure that.

Over the years, I've seen how women put up with it and let a guy control them, talk to them like they're worthless, and beat them. I've seen women with marks and bruises left on them. I want you to know you're not alone—just get out and talk to someone you trust. If you keep taking a guy back, he will do whatever he feels like. I was always told that if you allow him to do it once, he's just going to keep on doing it.

Sometimes you just have to let go. You think you can't, because you are so in love, but you will grow out of it eventually. If you're young, it's best to just be by yourself and grow up. It's hard, but if you're letting a guy control you, it's a waste of your time. More than that, it's dangerous—women who keep letting men abuse them can wind up dead. I feel so sad for women who hook up with these guys who think it's okay to put their hands on females and hurt them, but the women have to learn on their own and leave those relationships.

I can honestly say I've never been in an abusive relationship, and I don't ever want to be. Sometimes my boyfriends and I would play fight, but it wasn't anything where he was leaving marks on me. And it was nothing like I see with these guys who physically harm females in front of everyone and put women's lives at risk.

Sometimes I just sit and laugh to myself about these guys and other people who will betray you in life, because they will take you through hell and back without caring anything about you. If you have money, they're all in, but when you're down and out and need help, they've got no use for you. They'll laugh in your face and stab you in the back. Every chance I get, I expose guys for who they really are. I'm not mean—I just call it like I see it. Because of what I've seen, I still get mad when I see women in situations like the one I was in with Terryl. A guy sometimes realizes what he had after it's gone, but then it's too late. Men should treat their women right, because karma is real, and what you do comes back to you.

I'd never pretend to be perfect. I know I've made some bad mistakes, but I learned from them. I'm not the type to go on and on, holding on to someone who doesn't want to be held and who isn't willing to change. Men can have everything they could possibly want in their home, and they'll still ruin a happy home by sleeping around and acting like everything is cool. Ladies, you have to get it through your heads that you don't have to deal with this. You can be by yourself and move on. I know, because I've done it myself. I love myself too much to settle.

Looking back, I wish I'd known this sooner, but at the same time, the choices I made put me where I am today, and I'm happy now. I'm living for my children and doing what's best for me and them. The good part of all this is that women are always stronger. We know how to keep living when we are battling with other things. A guy can be on his last downfall and we can keep going while they seem to be needing us.

I salute you and stand up for you single mothers. It's hard, but you have to hold on. We're out here doing it all by ourselves with no help because some dudes won't show up for us. Sometimes it hurts, but you have to just keep on going and show your kids that you can make it. Nothing will ever change if you keep going backward. You can only better yourself if you're moving forward. Whether you realize it or not, there is always someone around you who is ready to support you through it all.

Don't ever let anyone make you feel like you're less, because you are always better than you think you are. Don't listen to people who don't have your best interests at heart, because at the end of the day, you're the one who has to live with yourself and the choices you are making. I won't lie—when you're in love or you love someone, it's hard. The hurt fades as time passes, but the more you love them, the longer that process takes. You have to wait it out, because if you don't move on, you will be hurt and broken.

I'm older now and have already been through too much. I loved Terryl but had to let him go because he played mind games with me and tried to bring me down so I would stay in a situation that wasn't good for me. I was really lowering my standards to be with him, but live and learn. I'm so happy now, and I'm happy for him as well. I was a moral person who gave him unconditional love. I never judged him, no matter how much his family judged me.

Through it all, I still had his back until he turned on me and spread rumors about me. But everyone in the city knew that he was no good for me, and I was just looking stupid. Well, lesson learned. I'm happy for him and I hope he gets what he wants out of life. It got so bad that his own mom finally took my side and began to love me, though I know the big draw was my daughter. Because of that, I forgave her for everything she'd put me through.

If you don't have kids, I want to tell you that you need to watch who you're sleeping with and have kids only with someone you know well and who will be a supportive part of your family. I can't complain—I love my kids, and every day I thank God for them. I went through hell and back to get here. I'm now supporting myself, doing hair, creating priceless moments with my kids and living each day like it's my last, and it feels good.

When you're alone and by yourself, everything is easier—it's such a relief. No stress, no drama, and you can make your own plans. You have peace and look at things differently than you ever have before. Keep learning, because things will happen in life and you can't just stay stuck where you are. You have to allow God to move in your life and go forward with faith. Things won't always be so bad, where you feel pain and don't know where to go. You have to open up and be willing to get healing. When you do, you will feel so much better, and you will no longer think about the pain or the person who hurt you, because you will be so happy in your life that nothing will matter but yourself and what's best for you. People can say all day long that they are there for you, but do you really know if they have the best intentions for you, or are they holding you up and delaying your blessings?

The woman I have become is powerful. I'm in a happy place with myself, and everything has changed for the better through prayer and focusing more on what my own life means. When you live with faith and belief in yourself, you grow. I'm so happy, and now that I'm an adult, there are things I won't allow in my life. The things I've gone through have made me a better woman and healed me from my past. I can now pick and choose how I want to deal with things, and I can walk away from bad situations so fast because I know my worth, and I'm not a teenager anymore. Nobody can treat me like a little girl or control me.

Now I'm with my soulmate, and everything I went through was worth it to get here. I committed to finding myself, and now I know who I am. You can be great as well. You need to learn who you are, what makes you happy, and what matters in life. You have to allow yourself to have standards and rules about how you want things to be. Don't let anybody treat you like less than you're worth. You are made to be whole, and the man you're with should see greatness in everything you do.

You are the shine, you are the glow. The light on you uplifts you—be kind and uplift others. Be different. Be supportive. Be inspired. You only need yourself to be the best you can be. Learn from my experience, and believe that you're worthy of the very best . . . because you are who you say you are!

www.ingramcontent.com/pod-product-compliance
Lightning Source LLC
LaVergne TN
LVHW091211080426
835509LV00006B/940